W9-BQM-727

MOVIE MAGIC
ANIMATION

BY SARA GREEN

BELLWETHER MEDIA • MINNEAPOLIS, MN

Blastoff! Discovery launches
a new mission: reading to learn.
Filled with facts and features, each
book offers you an exciting new
world to explore!

This edition first published in 2020 by Bellwether Media, Inc.

No part of this publication may be reproduced in whole or in
part without written permission of the publisher.
For information regarding permission, write to
Bellwether Media, Inc., Attention: Permissions Department,
6012 Blue Circle Drive, Minnetonka, MN 55343.

Library of Congress Cataloging-in-Publication Data

Names: Green, Sara, 1964- author.
Title: Animation / by Sara Green.
Description: Minneapolis, MN : Bellwether Media, Inc., 2020.
    | Series: Blastoff! Discovery. Movie Magic | Includes
    bibliographical references and index.
Identifiers: LCCN 2019000939 (print) | LCCN 2019001622
    (ebook) | ISBN 9781618915832 (ebook) | ISBN
    9781644870426 (hardcover : alk. paper)
Subjects: LCSH: Animation (Cinematography)-Juvenile
    literature.
Classification: LCC TR897.5 (ebook) | LCC TR897.5 .G745
    2020 (print) | DDC 777/.7-dc23
LC record available at https://lccn.loc.gov/2019000939

Editor: Betsy Rathburn   Designer: Brittany McIntosh

Printed in the United States of America, North Mankato, MN.

TABLE OF CONTENTS

INCREDIBLE!

The Metroville bank is under attack! The evil Underminer uses a huge drill to dig beneath the building. Then he sets off bombs! Can the Incredibles stop this bad guy before he destroys the city?

This is the opening scene in the animated film *Incredibles 2*. The movie is filled with action and excitement. But there are no live actors in the movie. The characters are drawings brought to life by animators!

Animated movies are made in many steps. Filmmakers took years to make *Incredibles 2*. Artists started by making simple drawings called storyboards. Then they created detailed artwork and models with computers.

Finally, animators used 3D computer technology to bring characters and settings to life. They also added lighting and special effects. With CGI, animators can make almost anything look real!

DEVELOPED BY DISNEY

Storyboards were first used by Disney in the 1930s. They have been used by many other companies ever since!

STORYBOARD

WHAT IS ANIMATION?

Animation is a type of art that makes drawings and objects appear to move. Artists called animators draw a series of pictures called **frames**. Each frame looks slightly different than the one before it.

The frames are played quickly, one after the other. This creates an **optical illusion**. People are actually looking at a series of still pictures. But their eyes see the objects moving!

FRAME COUNT

Each second of most animated movies has 24 frames. The large number of drawings helps make movements appear smooth.

ANIMATORS

Animation makes storytelling easier. Anything is possible! Filmmakers can make unusual characters come alive. Animated characters can do things that cannot be done in real life. For example, the characters travel inside the Internet in the 2018 movie *Ralph Breaks the Internet*.

Many animated films bring favorite comic book characters to life. Spider-Man first appeared in 1962 in a comic book. The filmmakers of *Spider-Man: Into the Spider-Verse* used animation to make audiences feel like they were entering a comic book world!

SULLEY

ATTENTION TO DETAIL

In the 2001 film *Monsters, Inc.*, Sulley has more than two million hairs on his body. Each one had to be created separately. It took animators about 12 hours to create each frame that featured Sulley!

HISTORY OF ANIMATION

Movies were invented in the 1890s. But people made animations long before then! The **zoetrope** was an animation device invented in 1834. It looked like a drum with slits cut into the sides. Pictures were arranged inside the drum. Spinning the drum made the pictures appear to move!

The first flip-book was made in 1868. Pictures appeared in slightly different locations on every page of a book. The pictures seemed to move when the pages were flipped quickly.

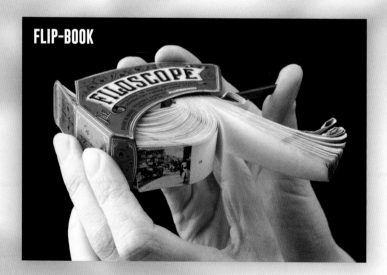

FLIP-BOOK

ZOETROPE

ANIMATOR LINING UP A CEL
WITH A BACKGROUND

14

Animated films were first made in the late 1800s. Back then, artists drew the same objects and backgrounds for each frame. This took a lot of time.

In 1915, Earl Hurd and John Bray invented **cel animation**. Artists paint one background on paper. Then they draw characters on separate cels, or pieces of clear plastic. The cels are placed on top of the background and photographed. This invention freed animators from having to redraw the background for each frame!

A DINOSAUR NAMED GERTIE

Gertie the Dinosaur is the first animated film to feature a dinosaur! A cartoonist named Winsor McCay made this 1914 film. He drew 10,000 images on rice paper to make the cartoon!

Stop-motion was another early animation method. An artist photographed an object, moved it a little, and then took another photo. This process was repeated over and over. When the photos were played back, the object appeared to move!

One of the first feature-length films made with stop-motion animation was the 1925 movie *The Lost World*. The filmmaker combined stop-motion dinosaurs with **live-action** scenes. Audiences had never seen anything like it before!

ISLE OF PUPPETS

Stop-motion is still a common animation technique today. The 2018 animated film *Isle of Dogs* was filmed in stop-motion. Filmmakers made 500 dog puppets and 500 human puppets for the stop-motion scenes.

THE LOST WORLD

ANIMATION PIONEER

Name: Walter "Walt" Disney
Born: December 5, 1901,
in Hermosa, Illinois
Known For: Animator who created
many famous characters and movies
such as *Snow White and the Seven
Dwarfs* (1937), *Pinocchio* (1940),
and *Cinderella* (1950), leading the
way for many Disney films in the future
Awards: Won 26 Academy Awards for animated films

*SNOW WHITE
AND THE SEVEN DWARFS*

Around the same time, the animator Walt Disney was developing his skills. Walt started his first film company in 1923. His **innovations** changed the animation **industry** forever. In 1932, the Disney company released its first full-color animated film called *Flowers and Trees.*

Five years later, Disney released its first full-length animated film, *Snow White and the Seven Dwarfs.* It broke **box office** records! *Pinocchio, Dumbo,* and other hit movies followed. Walt Disney set high standards for animated films. His ideas still inspire filmmakers today!

A CARTOON LEGEND

Mickey Mouse debuted in 1928 in several Disney cartoons. The most famous one was called *Steamboat Willie.*

Animation methods continued to advance. Computer animation began in the 1950s. At first, computer animations were only in **2D**. The first 3D animations appeared in films made in the 1970s. For example, a short 3D animation of the Death Star appeared in the 1977 film *Star Wars: Episode IV - A New Hope*.

The use of 3D animation skyrocketed during the late 1990s. In 1995, *Toy Story* was the first full-length computer-animated film ever made. It was an enormous hit!

3D ANIMATION IN *STAR WARS: EPISODE IV - A NEW HOPE*

TOY STORY

21

IN THEATERS NOW!

Today, many filmmakers have stopped creating 2D animated movies. Most animated films are made using 3D methods. These movies have lifelike characters, objects, and backgrounds. Animators are able to create detailed worlds that look much more real than older animation methods.

Some of today's most popular movies are made using 3D animation. Films like *Frozen* and *Incredibles 2* earned millions of dollars in ticket sales. Movies like these may be the future of animation!

LET IT SNOW

In the 2013 movie *Frozen*, Elsa creates her ice palace in 36 seconds. But each frame of this scene took animators about 30 hours to create!

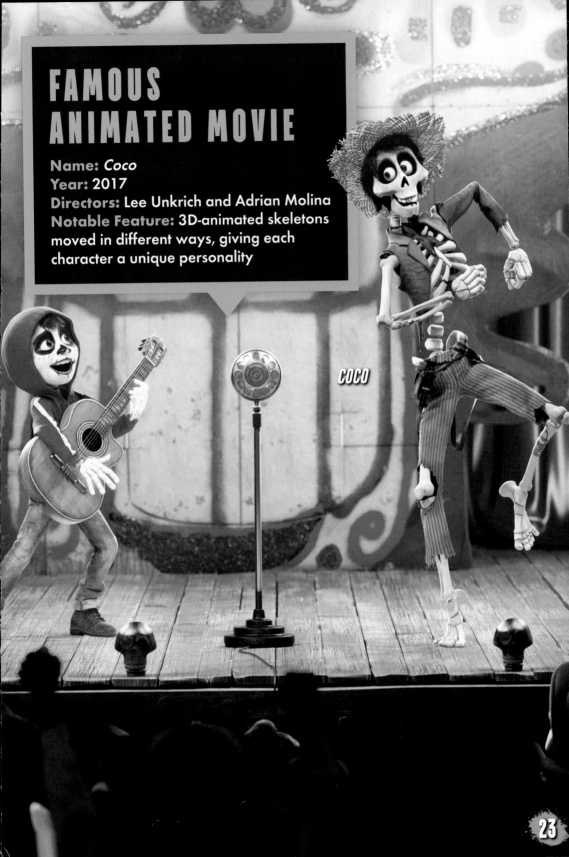

FAMOUS ANIMATED MOVIE

Name: *Coco*
Year: 2017
Directors: Lee Unkrich and Adrian Molina
Notable Feature: 3D-animated skeletons moved in different ways, giving each character a unique personality

COCO

MODERN ANIMATION MASTER

Name: Hayao Miyazaki
Born: January 5, 1941,
in Tokyo, Japan
Known For: Animator who created
many famous movies such as
Princess Mononoke (1997),
Spirited Away (2001), and *Ponyo* (2008)
Awards: Many awards for animation, including the Academy
Award for Best Animated Feature for *Spirited Away*

SPIRITED
AWAY

Traditional animation is more common outside of the United States. For example, many Japanese animation, or anime, films are created using 2D animation. This style of animation is known for its striking artwork.

One of the most famous Japanese animators is Hayao Miyazaki. His works are loved by moviegoers around the world. His 2001 film *Spirited Away* was a smash hit. More recently, the 2013 film *The Wind Rises* soared at box offices worldwide!

THE WIND RISES

Mixing live-action with animation is another common film method. Over time, animated penguins, fish, and mice have shared the screen with real actors! For example, the 2004 film *The SpongeBob SquarePants Movie* includes two worlds. Everything below the water is animated. Everything above the water is live-action.

Later, *The LEGO Movie* included a live-action ending. In the 2018 film *Christopher Robin*, an animated Winnie-the-Pooh travels through a live-action world!

THE AWARD GOES TO...

In 2001, the Academy Awards began including an award for Best Animated Feature. *Shrek* was the first movie to win this award.

WINNIE-THE-POOH IN
CHRISTOPHER ROBIN

COMING SOON

The popularity of 3D animated films is likely to remain strong. Audiences will continue seeing many favorite characters on the big screen.

Exciting advances in animation technology are also in the works. Some filmmakers are experimenting with **virtual reality**. This could change how people watch movies. Viewers will wear special VR headsets. This will allow them to become part of the movie. No matter the form, the magic of animation will continue to bring drawings to life!

FUTURE FEATURES

Animation fans can look forward to seeing many upcoming movies. The Minions and Scooby Doo will hit the big screen in the 2020s!

VIRTUAL
REALITY

GLOSSARY

2D—showing only length and height; 2D animations are usually created by hand.

3D—showing length, height, and depth; 3D animations are created with computers.

animators—artists who draw or use computers to create animations

box office—a measure of ticket sales sold by a film or other performance

cel animation—a type of animation in which characters and other details are drawn on clear plastic sheets and moved across a fixed background

CGI—artwork created by computers; CGI stands for computer-generated imagery.

frames—tiny parts of films; there are 24 frames per second in most movies.

industry—a group of businesses that provide a certain product

innovations—new methods or ideas

live-action—filmed using real actors

optical illusion—an image that is not what it seems to be

scene—the action in a single place and time in a film or play

special effects—a misleading image created for movies by using makeup, special props, camera systems, computer graphics, and other methods

stop-motion—a technique where objects are moved a tiny bit between frames; when the frames are played back, the objects appear to move on their own.

storyboards—sets of drawings that show what will happen in a film or television show

virtual reality—a pretend world created by a computer; users wear special headsets to enter and move around in this world.

zoetrope—an early animation toy shaped like a drum with slits on the side; pictures on the inside appeared to move when the drum was spun.

TO LEARN MORE

AT THE LIBRARY

Horn, Geoffrey M. *Movie Animation*. Milwaukee, Wisc.: Gareth Stevens Publishing, 2007.

Levete, Sarah. *Maker Projects for Kids Who Love Animation*. New York, N.Y.: Crabtree Publishing Company, 2016.

Wilkinson Saldaña, Zoë. *Filming Stop-Motion Animation*. Ann Arbor, Mich.: Cherry Lake Publishing, 2018.

ON THE WEB

FACTSURFER

Factsurfer.com gives you a safe, fun way to find more information.

1. Go to www.factsurfer.com.

2. Enter "animation" into the search box and click 🔍.

3. Select your book cover to see a list of related web sites.

INDEX